Merry Things to Make

Christmas Fun and Crafts

by Diane Cherkerzian and Colleen Van Blaricom

Illustrated by Allan Eitzen and Anita Louise

Boyds Mills Press

Copyright © 1999 by Boyds Mills Press
All rights reserved

Published by Bell Books
Boyds Mills Press
A Highlights company
815 Church Street
Honesdale, Pennsylvania 18431
Printed in the United States of America

Publisher Cataloging-in-Publication Data
Available upon request
ISBN 1-56397-838-5

First edition, 1999
The text of this book is set in 12-point New Century Schoolbook.

10 9 8 7 6 5 4 3 2 1

Mrs. Claus's famous fudge, a 2,000-year-old game gift, elves, santas, angels, and oodles of ornaments . . .

These are just a few of the great things you'll find in *Merry Things to Make*. This book features step-by-step instructions and colorful illustrations. In need of a centerpiece, a toy, or a wreath? A quick glance at the subject index will point you in the right direction.

All of the projects in *Merry Things to Make* can be made from inexpensive items found around the house. You'll need cooking items like butter and marshmallows, as well as crafting things like construction paper, aluminum foil, string, milk cartons, cardboard tubes, and tree twigs.

Before you begin a project:

- Read through all the directions from start to finish.
- Gather all the materials you'll need.
- Cover your work area with newspaper and yourself with a smock or a man's old shirt.

As you go through each activity:

- Ask a grown-up if you need help.
- Add your own creative touches to everything you make!
- Clean up when you're finished.

Have a Happy Holiday!

This elf can be a tree ornament.

Santa's Helper

You will need:
- a peanut in its shell
- a felt-tip marker
- a pipe cleaner
- cotton balls
- glue
- red felt
- scissors
- a paper clip

3. Draw a face on the peanut with the marker. Glue on some cotton for a beard.

To make Santa's Helper:

1. Cut out a long, thin triangle from felt as shown.

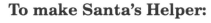

4. Cut the pipe cleaner into four pieces, each about 2 inches long. Glue them onto the peanut for arms and legs.

2. Glue the felt to one end of the peanut. Glue a bit of cotton under the piece of felt.

5. Bend the paper clip into a loop, and poke it through the felt hat for a hanger.

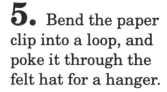

This jolly Santa Claus is sure to brighten up your Christmas tree.

Eggshell Santa Ornament

2. For Santa's coat, paint the bottom of the eggshell red. Paint on a red hat and a red nose. Let the eggshell dry. Draw Santa's eyes with the black marker.

You will need:

an egg

a paintbrush

a black marker

red paint

glue

ribbon

cotton balls

To make the Eggshell Santa Ornament:

1. Poke a small hole in the bottom of the egg, just big enough to let the egg flow out. You may have to prick the yolk so it will flow out. Rinse the inside of the egg, and let it dry.

3. Using the cotton balls, glue fur trim around Santa's hat. Then glue on a mustache and a beard. Glue a loop of ribbon to the top of your ornament so you can hang it on your tree.

Add a twinkle to your tree.

Shining Stars

You will need:
- paper
- a pencil
- waxed paper
- ribbon
- glue
- glitter

3. Spread glue on a piece of yarn and use it to outline the star on the waxed paper.

To make Shining Stars:

1. Draw a star on a piece of paper.

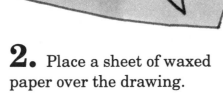

4. While the glue is still wet, sprinkle glitter onto the piece of yarn and let it dry overnight.

2. Place a sheet of waxed paper over the drawing.

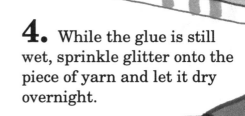

5. Peel the star off the waxed paper, and tie on a piece of ribbon so you can hang the star in a window or on your tree.

6. Make other ornaments in the shape of bells, trees, candy canes, and hearts.

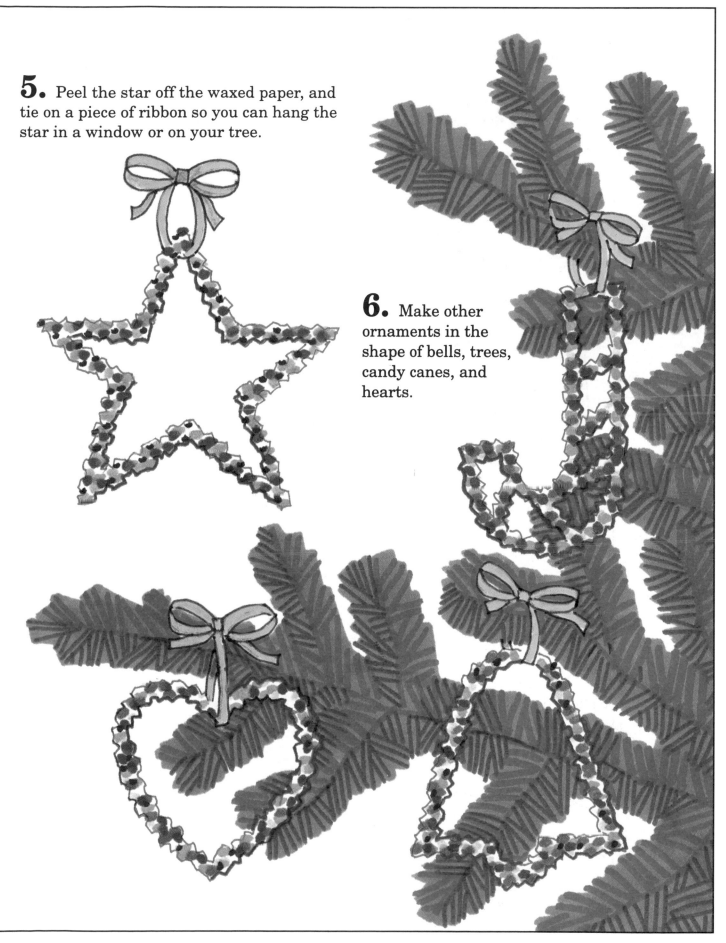

*Make lots of angels in different colors
to brighten up your Christmas tree.*

Tissue-Paper Angel

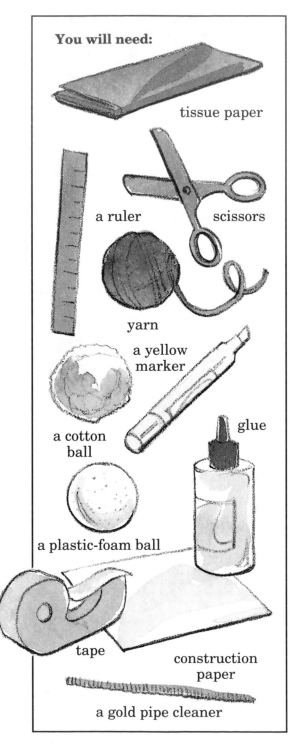

You will need:

tissue paper

a ruler

scissors

yarn

a yellow marker

a cotton ball

glue

a plastic-foam ball

tape

construction paper

a gold pipe cleaner

To make the Tissue-Paper Angel:

1. To make the angel's wings, cut a piece of tissue paper 6 inches by 12 inches. Fold it like a fan. The folds should be parallel to the 6-inch side of the paper. Each pleat should be a ½ inch wide.

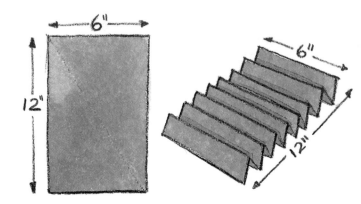

2. Cut a piece of yarn 10 inches long. Tie it tightly around the center of the wings. Fluff out the wings.

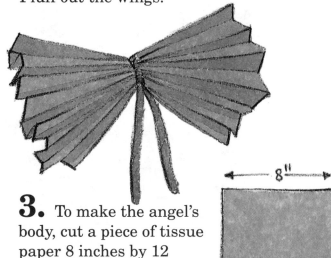

3. To make the angel's body, cut a piece of tissue paper 8 inches by 12 inches. Follow the folding instructions in step 1.

4. Tightly tie a piece of yarn about one-third of the way down the body. Clip the yarn ends. Fluff out the tissue paper to make a headpiece and skirt. Place the wings on top of the body, yarn facing down. Tie the wings to the body. Clip the yarn ends.

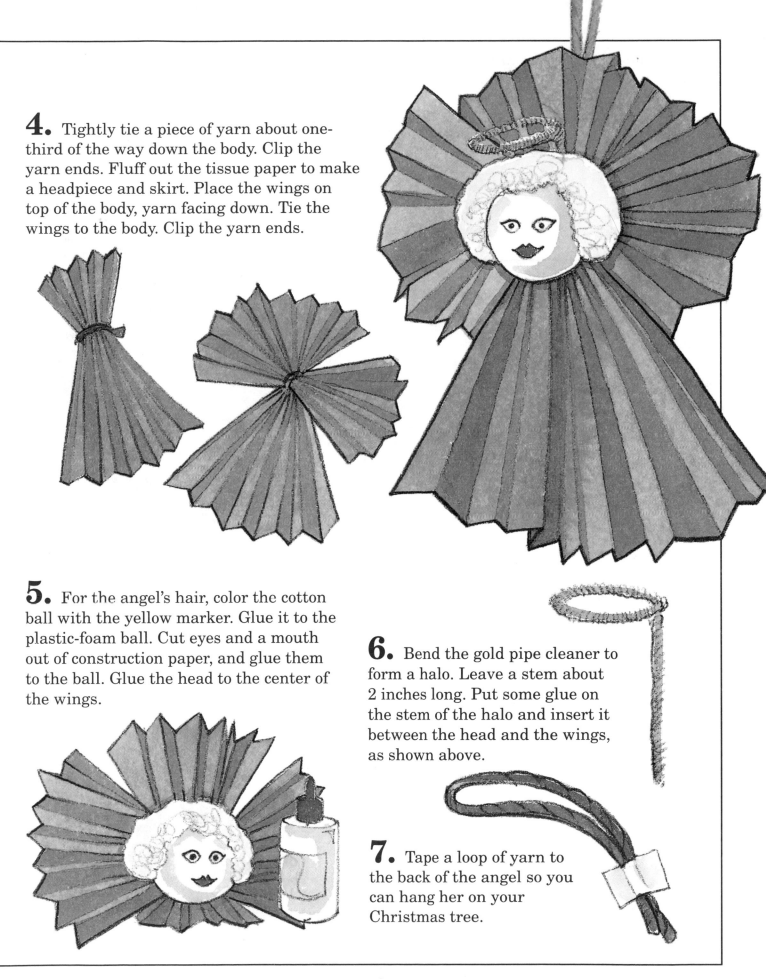

5. For the angel's hair, color the cotton ball with the yellow marker. Glue it to the plastic-foam ball. Cut eyes and a mouth out of construction paper, and glue them to the ball. Glue the head to the center of the wings.

6. Bend the gold pipe cleaner to form a halo. Leave a stem about 2 inches long. Put some glue on the stem of the halo and insert it between the head and the wings, as shown above.

7. Tape a loop of yarn to the back of the angel so you can hang her on your Christmas tree.

9

Make lots of these quick and easy ornaments to hang on your tree.

Candy-Cane Ornament

You will need:

a fat white pipe cleaner

glue

scissors

red ribbon

2. Wind the ribbon at a slant down the length of the pipe cleaner.

To make the Candy-Cane Ornament:

1. Bend the pipe cleaner into the shape of a candy cane. Glue one end of the ribbon to the curved end of the pipe cleaner. Hold it in place till it sticks.

3. When you reach the end, trim off the extra ribbon and secure the end with glue.

Create one-of-a-kind snowflakes to hang on your Christmas tree.

Berry-Basket Snowflakes

You will need:

scissors

a paper plate

berry baskets

glue

yarn

a paintbrush

glitter

2. Glue two snowflakes together diagonally. Leave them their natural color, or paint them white; then let them dry.

3. Sprinkle glitter onto a paper plate. Brush both sides of the snowflake with glue, and dip it in the glitter. Let it dry. Tie a loop of yarn through the snowflake to make a hanger.

To make Berry-Basket Snowflakes:

1. Cut out the bottoms of the berry baskets. Snip away pieces of the baskets to make snowflake designs.

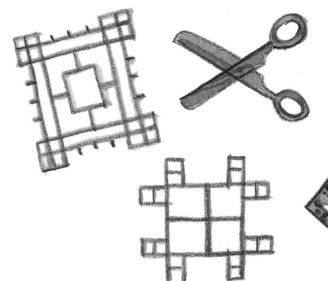

11

These bells will jingle merrily on your Christmas tree or on a doorknob.

Egg-Carton Jingle Bells

You will need:

scissors

two jingle bells

yarn

sequins

aluminum foil

an egg carton

glue

2. Poke a hole in the top of each cup. Thread a length of yarn through each jingle bell. Thread the yarn through the hole inside each cup to the outside. (The jingle bell will be inside the cup, and the yarn will come out the top.) Tie the yarn in a bow to hold the two cups together.

To make Egg-Carton Jingle Bells:

1. Cut two cups from the egg carton. Trim the edges. Cover the cups with aluminum foil.

3. Decorate the egg-carton bells with sequins.

Christmas Tree Centerpiece

You will need:
- an 18-by-12-inch piece of poster board
- four cardboard paper towel tubes
- scissors • poster paint • glue
- tape • a paintbrush

To make the Christmas Tree Centerpiece:

1. From poster board, cut a very large half-circle and bend it to form a cone. Tape the cone so it will stay in shape. (If necessary, cut around the bottom edge of the cone so that it will stand up straight.)

2. Flatten the cardboard tubes and cut each into ½-inch slices. Open the slices slightly so they are football-shaped. Glue the slices onto the cone so they are close together.

3. When the whole tree is covered with cardboard slices, let it dry, and then paint it. Glue on small decorations made from tissue paper, felt, or beads.

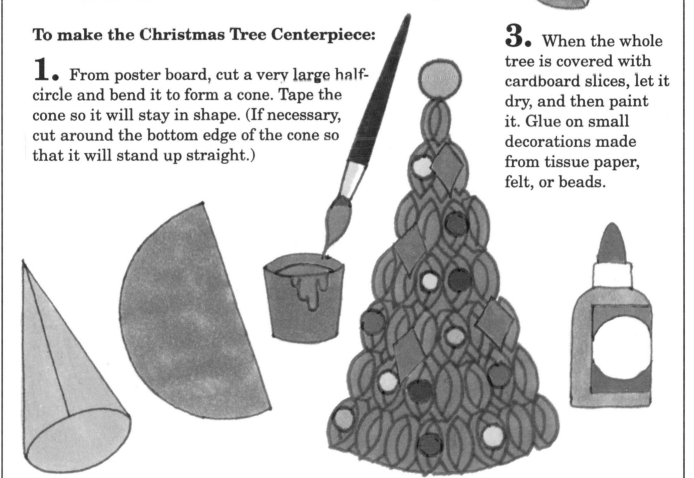

These cheerful candles will glow throughout the holiday season.

Christmas

14

You will need:

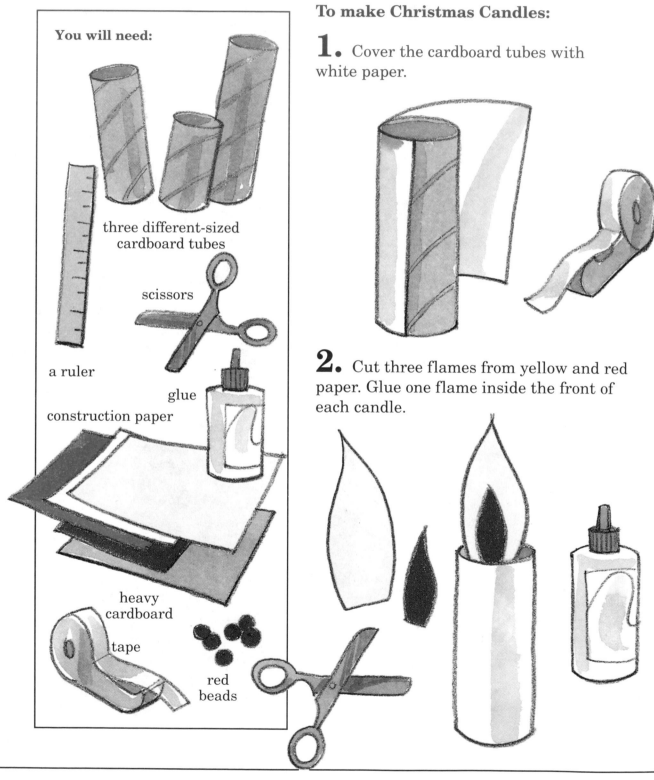

three different-sized cardboard tubes

scissors

a ruler

glue

construction paper

heavy cardboard

tape

red beads

To make Christmas Candles:

1. Cover the cardboard tubes with white paper.

2. Cut three flames from yellow and red paper. Glue one flame inside the front of each candle.

Candles

3. Cut a 6-inch circle from the heavy cardboard. Glue the candles in the center.

5. Glue on some red beads for holly berries among the leaves.

4. Cut holly leaves from green paper. Glue them all around the base.

*Display your elves as a merry
bunch of Christmas carolers.*

Pinecone Elves

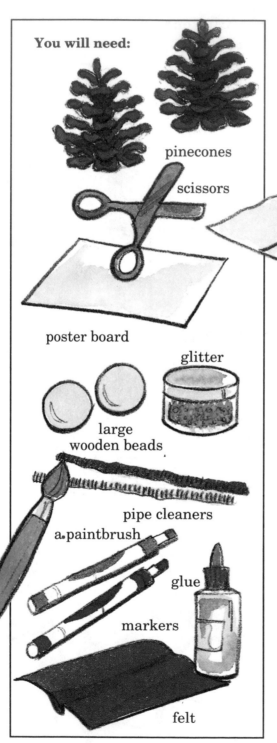

You will need:

pinecones

scissors

poster board

glitter

large
wooden beads

pipe cleaners

a paintbrush

glue

markers

felt

To make Pinecone Elves:

1. Spread newspaper over your work area. Brush some glue on the pinecones. Sprinkle with glitter, and let them dry.

2. Using the markers, draw faces on the wooden beads. Twist the pipe cleaners into the shape of ski caps. Glue them onto the wooden beads. Then glue the beads onto the pinecones, and let them dry.

3. To make the elves' arms, wrap one pipe cleaner around each pinecone. Trim the pipe cleaners if they're too long, and loop the ends to make hands.

4. Make music books out of folded rectangles of poster board, and glue them between the elves' hands.

5. To make scarves, cut strips of felt, and tie them around the elves' necks.

This Nativity scene made out of milk cartons will fill your house with true Christmas spirit.

Nativity Scene

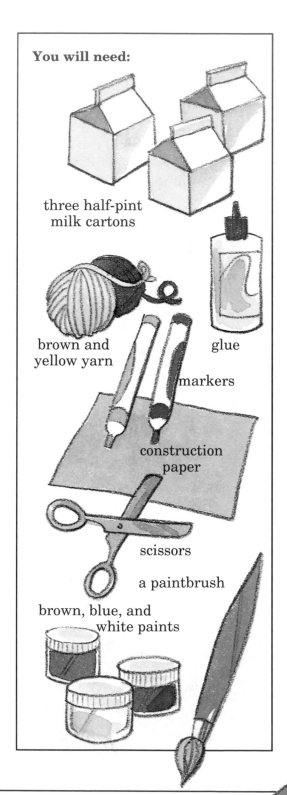

You will need:

three half-pint milk cartons

brown and yellow yarn

glue

markers

construction paper

scissors

a paintbrush

brown, blue, and white paints

To make the Nativity Scene:

1. Cut off the top portions of the three milk cartons, as shown. Throw away the bottoms.

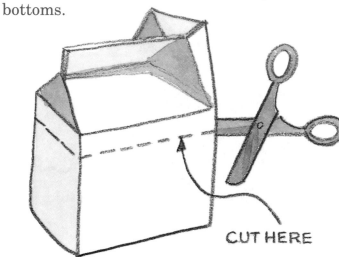

CUT HERE

2. With the spout open, paint one of the cartons brown for Joseph. You may need to add a bit of dishwashing liquid to the paint to make it stick. Paint the second carton blue for Mary and the third carton white for the Baby Jesus.

3. For the faces, cut three squares of paper about twice as large as the spout opening. Rub glue around the inside of each spout. Poke a square through the back of each carton so that the spout is filled with the paper. Draw a face on each with markers. Glue on yarn for hair and a mustache and beard for Joseph.

4. Cut hands out of paper, and glue them onto Joseph and Mary.

5. Glue a square of paper over the backs of Joseph and Mary.

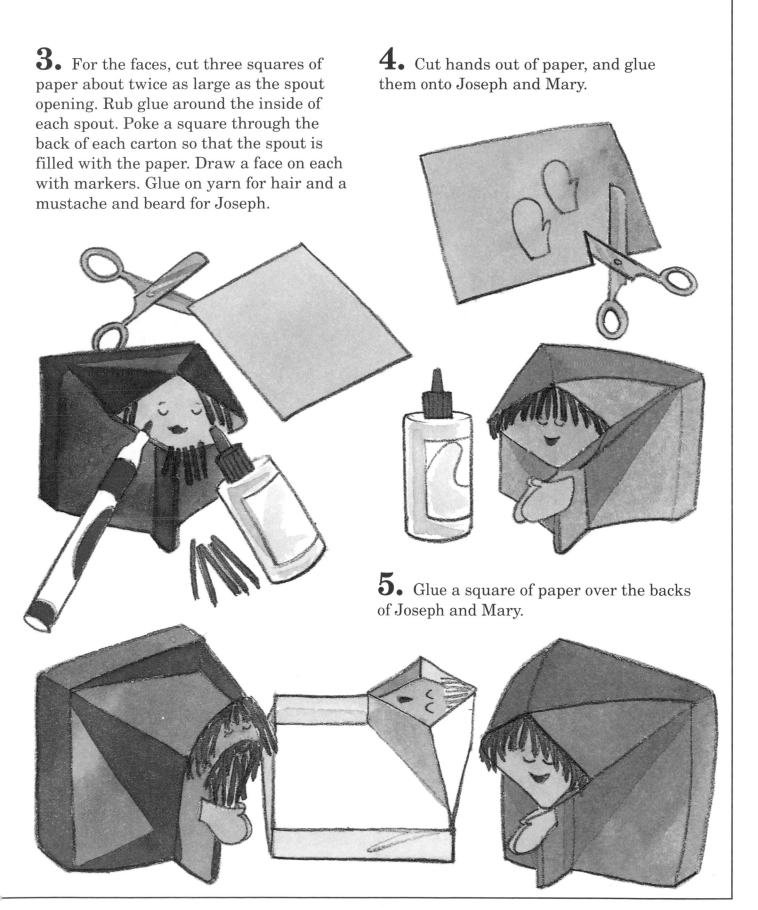

Wouldn't you love to live in such a "sweet" cottage?

Santa Claus's Cottage

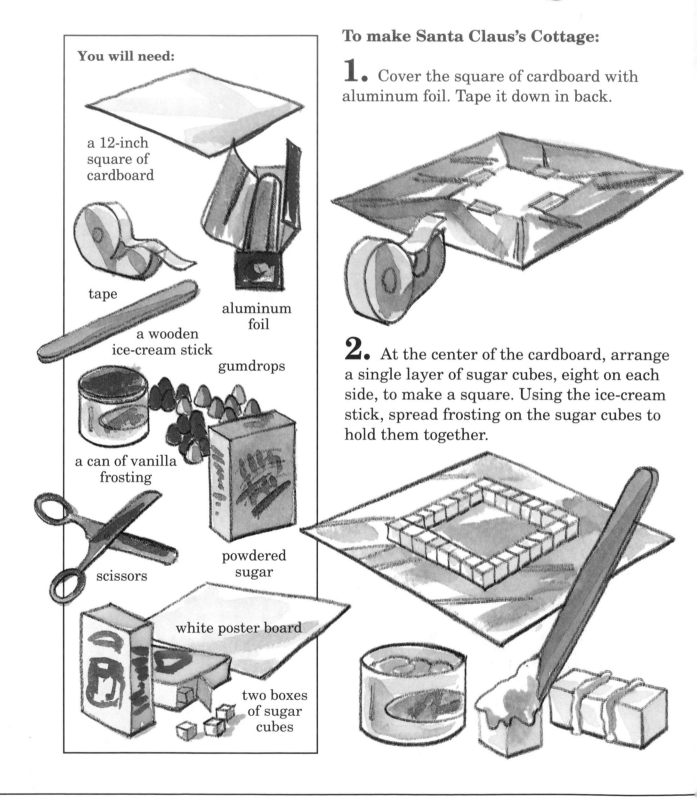

You will need:

a 12-inch square of cardboard

tape

aluminum foil

a wooden ice-cream stick

gumdrops

a can of vanilla frosting

scissors

powdered sugar

white poster board

two boxes of sugar cubes

To make Santa Claus's Cottage:

1. Cover the square of cardboard with aluminum foil. Tape it down in back.

2. At the center of the cardboard, arrange a single layer of sugar cubes, eight on each side, to make a square. Using the ice-cream stick, spread frosting on the sugar cubes to hold them together.

3. Continue to build Santa Claus's cottage, layer by layer, following the diagrams below.

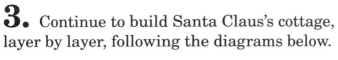

FRONT   SIDE

WINDOW   WINDOW   WINDOW

DOOR

BACK

4. As you are building up the walls, leave spaces for the door and windows, as shown in the diagrams. To support the tops of the door and windows, cut thin strips of poster board slightly larger than the openings. Lay the strips across the openings. Continue layering sugar cubes on top of the strips.

strip of poster board

5. Decorate the turrets on top of the cottage with gumdrops. Place yellow gumdrops in the windows to look like candles. Stack green gumdrops in front of the cottage to look like bushes. Spread frosting on the trees and on top of the cottage for snow. Sprinkle powdered sugar around the cottage to look like more snow.

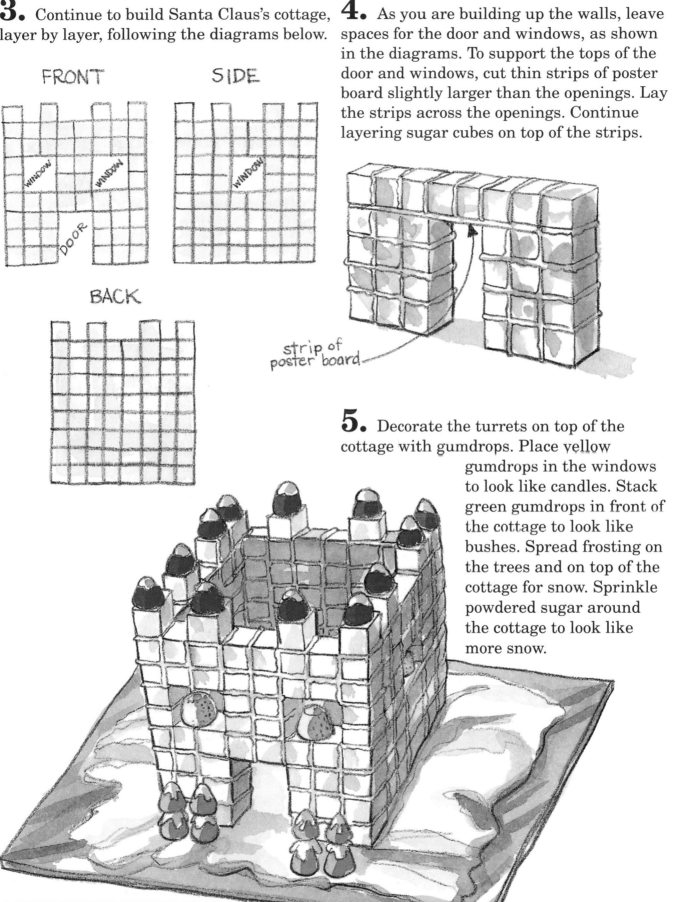

This little Christmas tree will fit in any room.

Tabletop Tree

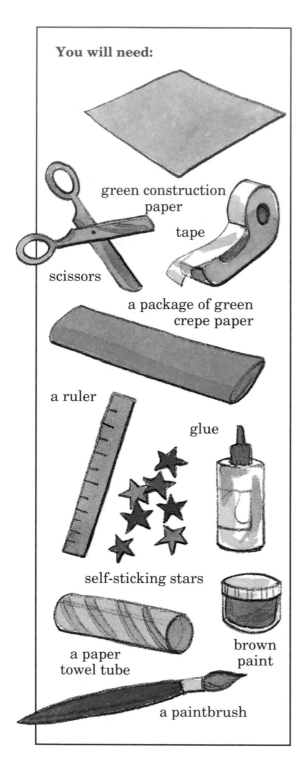

You will need:

green construction paper

scissors

tape

a package of green crepe paper

a ruler

glue

self-sticking stars

a paper towel tube

brown paint

a paintbrush

To make the Tabletop Tree:

1. Cut a half-circle from the green construction paper. Roll it into a cone, and tape it shut. If the bottom of the cone does not lie flat, you may need to trim it with scissors.

2. Cut the package of green crepe paper into 2-inch strips, as shown.

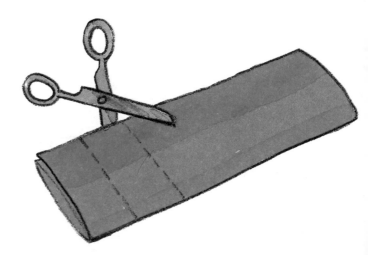

3. Cut slits halfway up each strip, as shown. Open up the strips.

5. Continue gluing strips around the cone, overlapping rows. Cover the entire cone. For the tree trunk, cut the paper towel tube to about 6 inches long. Paint it brown, and let it dry. Glue the tree on top of the trunk.

6. Decorate the tree with the stars.

4. Starting at the bottom edge, glue the unfringed half of a strip to the cone. The fringed half will hang down.

23

Perch St. Nick on a shelf or fireplace mantel so that his legs hang down.

Sitting St. Nick

You will need:

a cardboard tube

a small white pom-pon

pink, red, white, and black felt

glue

a ruler

scissors

a cotton ball

pinking shears (optional)

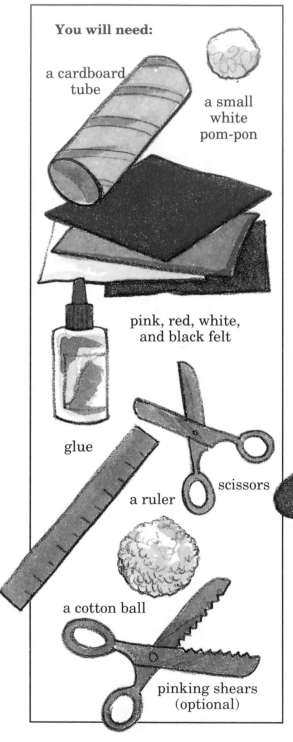

To make Sitting St. Nick:

1. To make St. Nick's face, glue pink felt on the top half of the cardboard tube. To make his coat, glue red felt on the bottom half of the tube.

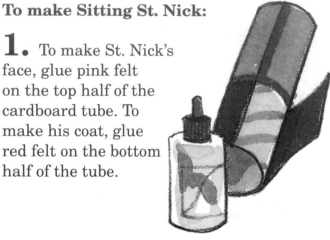

2. To make St. Nick's arms, cut a piece of red felt 1 inch wide by 10 inches long. Cut two mittens out of black felt, and glue them to the ends of the red felt. Using the pinking shears or scissors, cut two pieces of white felt for the cuffs. Glue them around St. Nick's wrists.

3. Glue the middle of the arms around the back of the cardboard tube. Let the arms hang down at the sides.

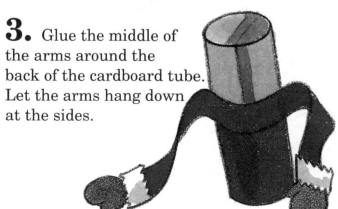

4. To make St. Nick's legs, cut two pieces of red felt 1 inch wide by 6 inches long. Cut two boots out of black felt, and glue them to the ends of the red felt. Using the pinking shears or scissors, cut two pieces of white felt for the cuffs. Glue them around St. Nick's ankles. Glue the legs to the inside front of the cardboard tube.

5. Using the pinking shears or scissors, cut a strip of white felt for St. Nick's belt. Glue it around his waist, as shown on the right. Cut a belt buckle out of black felt, and glue it to the belt. Cut two buttons out of white felt, and glue them onto St. Nick's jacket. Cut eyes, a nose, a mustache, and a mouth out of felt. Glue them onto St. Nick's face.

6. To make his hair, spread out the cotton ball and glue it around the top of the tube.

7. To make St. Nick's hat, cut a half-circle out of red felt. Roll it into a cone shape, and glue the edges together. To make a cuff for the hat, cut a strip of white felt with the pinking shears or scissors, and glue it around the bottom of the hat. Glue the white pom-pon on top. Then glue the hat on top of St. Nick's hair.

25

Hang this with care, and Santa's sure to be there.

Christmas Stocking

You will need:

- a pencil
- scissors
- white glue
- glitter
- green yarn
- newspaper
- two pieces of red felt (each about 8½ by 11 inches)
- a sewing needle with a large eye
- an 8½-by-11-inch sheet of plain white paper

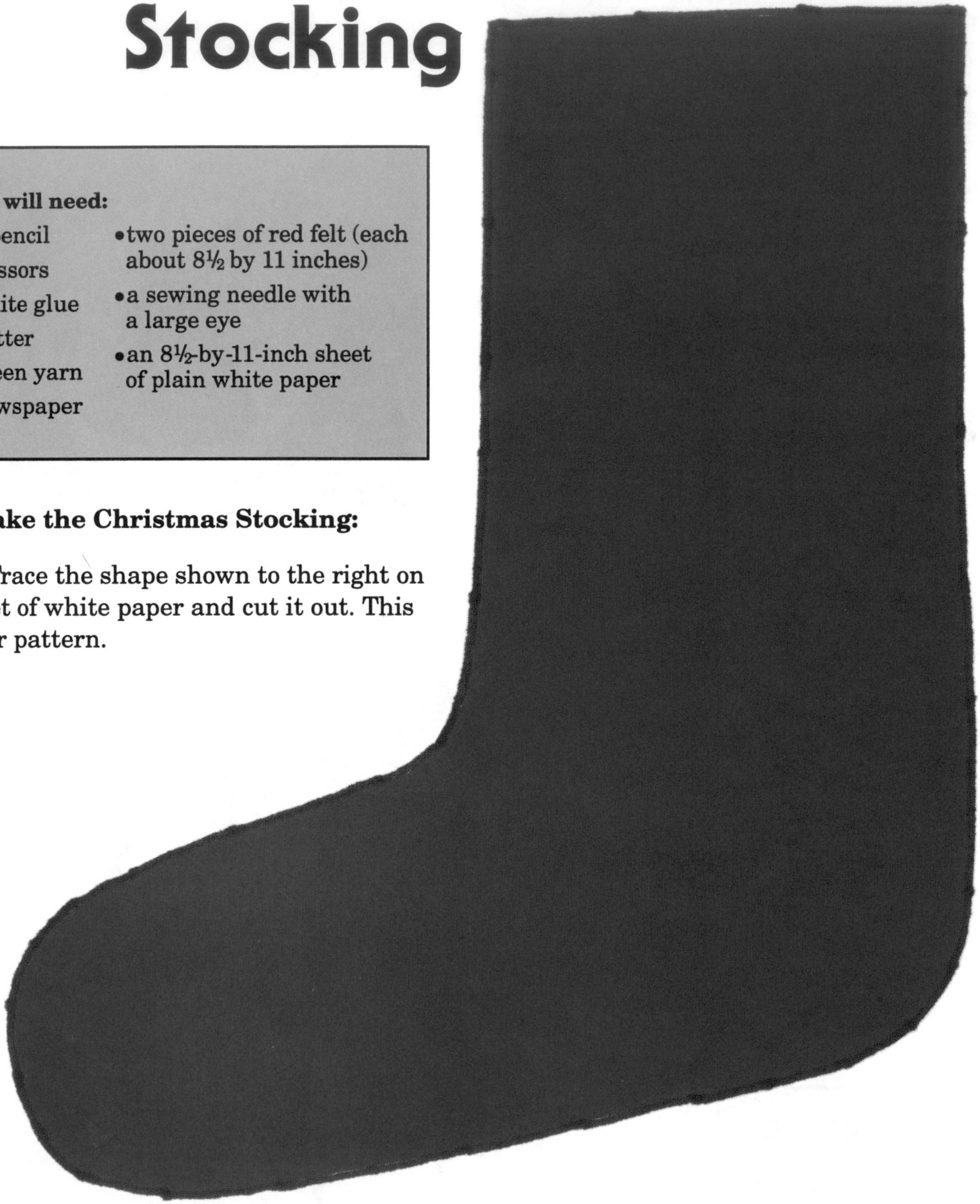

To make the Christmas Stocking:

1. Trace the shape shown to the right on a sheet of white paper and cut it out. This is your pattern.

2. Place the pattern on a piece of felt, trace the shape, and cut it out. Do the same with the other piece of felt.

3. Thread a long piece of yarn through the needle, and tie a knot at the ends of the yarn. Sew the two pieces of felt together, using a wide overcast stitch as shown.

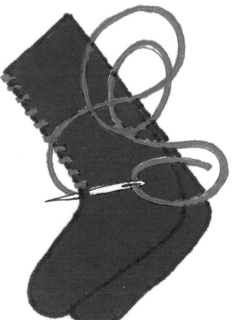

Cover your work area with newspaper.

4. Write your name with glue on the stocking, then sprinkle glitter over the glue. Pick up the stocking so that the extra glitter falls off.

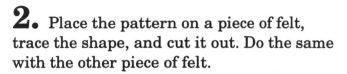

5. To hang up your stocking, make a loop by cutting a thin, 4-inch strip of felt. Fold the strip in half, and stitch or staple it to the top of the stocking.

This Christmas wreath is sure to bring smiles to all who see it.

Smile Wreath

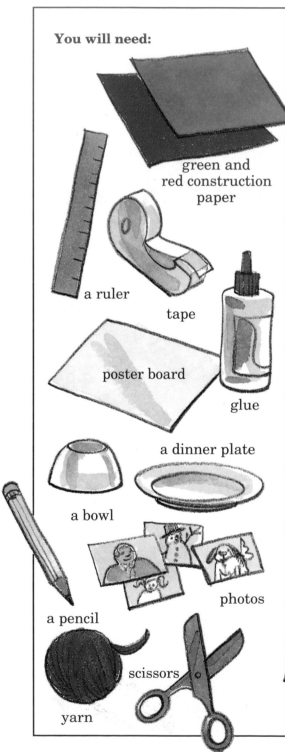

You will need:

green and red construction paper

a ruler

tape

poster board

glue

a dinner plate

a bowl

photos

a pencil

scissors

yarn

To make the Smile Wreath:

1. Overlap two pieces of green paper so that you have a 12-inch square. Tape the papers together both front and back. Glue the green paper to a piece of poster board.

2. Place the dinner plate, upside down, on the square. Lightly trace around it. Lay the bowl upside down in the middle of the circle, and trace around it. Draw scallops on the outside and inside edges. Cut out the wreath.

28

3. Choose some small photos of yourself, your family, your pets, and anything else you'd like, and glue them to your wreath. Save room for a bow and some holly berries.

4. Cut a bow and holly berries out of red paper, and glue them on.

5. Tape a loop of yarn to the back of your wreath so you can hang it up.

Tape your stained-glass design to a window for the light to shine through.

Stained-Glass Window

You will need:

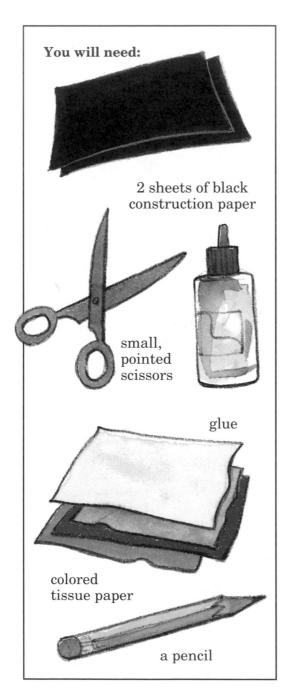

2 sheets of black construction paper

small, pointed scissors

glue

colored tissue paper

a pencil

To make the Stained-Glass Window:

1. Place two sheets of black construction paper together. Fold them in half. Using the pencil, draw a design on one half of the paper, as shown. Draw some of the design on the fold.

FOLD HERE

FOLD

2. Cut out the design with the scissors. **You may want to ask an adult for help using the scissors.**

3. Open up the two papers, and set one aside. On the other paper, glue small pieces of different-colored tissue paper over every cutout. The pieces of tissue paper should be slightly larger than the cutouts they are covering. Put the glue on the black paper, being careful not to get it on the tissue paper, and gently press the tissue paper over the glue.

4. Take the paper that you set aside earlier, and glue it on top of the paper to which you glued the tissue paper. Match the cutouts exactly.

GLUE

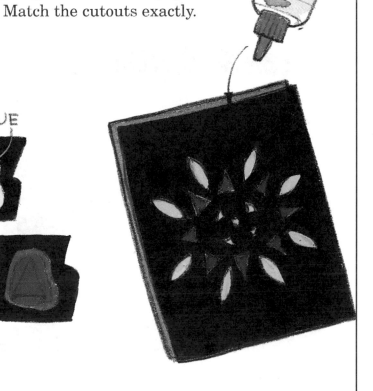

Stained-Glass

Shepherd

You will need:

- a sheet of plain white paper
- two sheets of black construction paper
- colored tissue paper or cellophane
- a pencil   • scissors   • paper clips
- rubber cement glue

To make the Stained-Glass Shepherd:

1. On a white sheet of paper, trace the pattern on the opposite page. Be sure to make the black lines thick enough.

2. Label each white section with the name of the color you want it to be.

3. Carefully cut out all of the sections that will be colored. Be sure not to cut through any black lines, and don't damage the cutout "colored" sections—you will need them later.

4. Using paper clips, secure the sheet of white paper you have cut out to a sheet of black paper. Trace the shape of the white paper on the black sheet. Again, cut out the sections that will be colored, leaving just the black lines. Repeat this step using the second sheet of black paper.

5. Trace the "colored" sections you cut out from the white paper onto the colored tissue or cellophane.

6. When you cut out the tissue or cellophane pieces, allow a ½-inch border around all sides of each piece so that they are a bit larger than the paper cutouts.

7. Carefully brush rubber cement on the lines of one sheet of black paper. Secure the colored cutouts to that sheet. Allow the glue to dry. Apply glue to the edges and lines of the second sheet of black paper. Place it over the first sheet so that it matches exactly.

Once dry, place the Stained-Glass Shepherd in a sunny window, or attach a string to the shepherd and hang it on your tree.

A fun "twist" for the holiday season.

Deer Knob

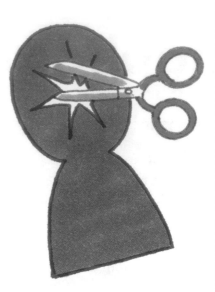

2. Poke a hole in the center of the circle with the scissors, then cut a few slashes around the hole as shown.

To make the Deer Knob:

1. Draw the shape of a reindeer's head and neck on the large piece of felt and cut it out.

3. Cut ears, eyes, antlers, and a mouth from scraps of felt. Glue them to the reindeer. Once it's dry, decorate your (or someone else's) doorknob.

This mouse makes a great stocking stuffer.

Christmas Mouse Magnet

You will need:
- felt
- scissors
- half of a walnut shell
- glue
- magnetic tape (found in hobby shops or hardware stores)

To make the Christmas Mouse Magnet:

1. From the felt, cut out the mouse's feet, eyes, ears, tail, and whiskers.

2. Glue the pieces of felt to the walnut shell as shown.

3. Cut a strip of the magnetic tape and glue it to the bottom of the magnet.

To Minnie

Rudolph Puppet

You will need:

construction paper

scissors

a pencil

an old pair of pantyhose

glue

a clothes hanger

a large red pom-pon

To make the Rudolph Puppet:

1. Bend the clothes hanger as shown in the diagram. **You may want an adult to help you with this.**

2. Cut one leg off the pantyhose, and slip it over the hanger. The toe section of the stocking should be at the nose of the puppet. Tie a knot in the end of the stocking where you will hold the puppet.

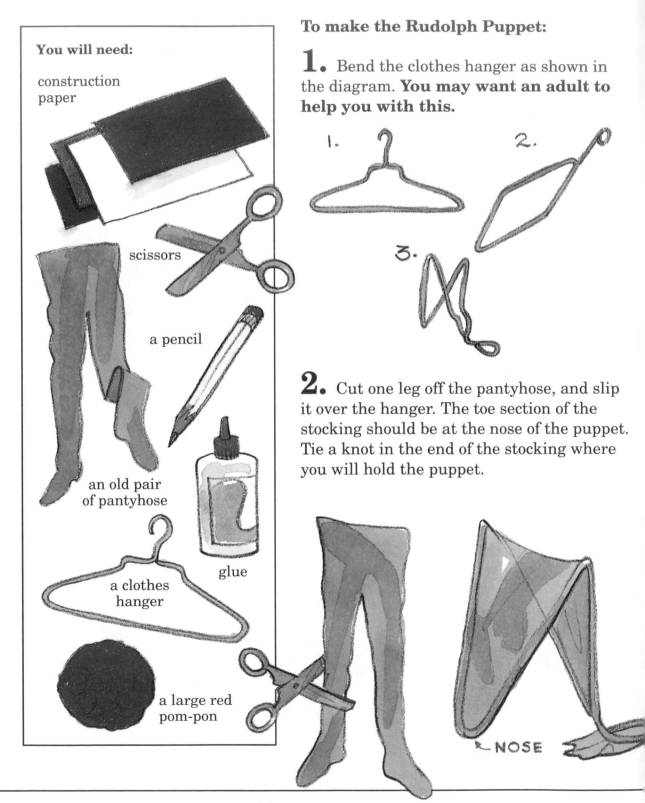

NOSE

3. To make the antlers, trace around your hands on red construction paper. Cut them out. Glue them on the pantyhose.

4. Draw and cut out ears and eyes from construction paper. Glue them on. Then glue on the red pom-pon for Rudolph's nose.

Here's a warm, soft snowman you can cuddle up to!

Sock Snowman

You will need:

a white sock

scissors

cotton balls

black felt

scrap fabric

glue

yarn

To make the Sock Snowman:

1. Stuff the sock with cotton balls up to the cuff. Fold the cuff down to make the snowman's hat. The heel of the sock will be the snowman's face.

2. Make a scarf by tying a strip of the fabric underneath the heel, separating the snowman's head from his body.

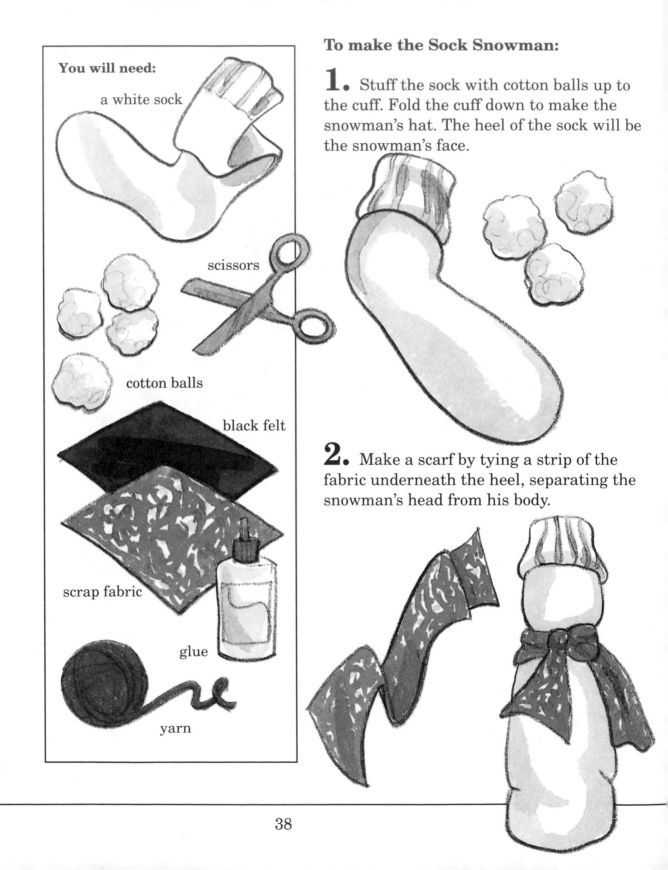

3. Cut eyes, a nose, a mouth, and buttons out of black felt, and glue them on the snowman.

4. To make a tassel for the top of the hat, loop some yarn as shown. Tie one end with a small piece of yarn, and glue it inside the top of the hat. Clip the ends that are hanging down.

Make a set for yourself and one for a friend. It's a great gift.

Knucklebones

This game was invented more than two thousand years ago by the Greeks. There are many different ways to play, including throwing the highest roll, throwing four different faces, four identical faces, or throwing them up in the air and catching them on the back of your hand.

You will need:
- ½ cup flour
- ¼ cup salt
- ¼ cup water
- 2 teaspoons glycerin or olive oil
- a toothpick
- a spoon
- a mixing bowl
- a table knife
- a wire rack
- a coffee mug
- a ruler

To make Knucklebones:

1. Stir together the flour and salt in a bowl.

2. Mix the water and glycerin (or olive oil) in the coffee mug.

3. Gradually add enough liquid to the dough so it comes cleanly away from the sides of the bowl.

4. Roll the dough with your hands until it is a very smooth sausage-shaped roll, about 1½ inches wide and 6 inches long. Use the knife to mark twelve ½-inch pieces.

5. Cut off one piece and mold it until you have a shape with four flat sides. Cut and shape the other pieces the same way.

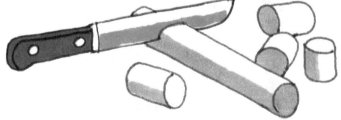

6. Make a long line on one side of each piece with a toothpick.

7. Turn the pieces to the second side and poke three holes in each with a toothpick.

8. Turn the pieces over to the third side and make four horizontal lines as shown.

9. Turn the pieces to the fourth side and make six holes in each piece.

10. Carefully place the pieces on a wire rack and leave them in a warm, dry place for a few days until they are dry. DO NOT dry the pieces in an oven because they will get puffy, and it is important that they stay flat.

Jolly Santa

You will need:
- glue
- cotton balls
- scissors
- construction paper
- white yarn
- tape
- a cardboard bathroom tissue tube
- red, white, and brown crepe paper

2. Stretch red crepe paper over the cotton, letting the bottom hang as the lower part of the coat. Cut out and glue on black paper buttons and a belt and a yellow buckle.

To make the Jolly Santa:

1. Cover the lower part of the cardboard tube with red crepe paper. Tape two cotton balls on the upper part of the tube for a tummy.

3. For the head, cover four cotton balls with white crepe paper. Glue the ends of the paper to the top of the tube. Cut out and glue on blue paper eyes and a red mouth. Glue on bits of white yarn for hair, whiskers, and a moustache.

4. Stretch out two cotton balls lengthwise to form arms. Cover each piece of cotton with red crepe paper. Glue the ends together.

5. Cut out and glue on four black paper mittens, two for each hand. Glue the arms to the body.

6. For the hat, glue red crepe paper around the head to fit. Turn up the brim, twist the tassel end, and add cotton trim as shown.

7. To make a bag of toys, cover cotton with brown crepe paper. Use a piece of yarn to tie it closed, forming a loop to glue to Santa's hand.

43

Angel Puppet

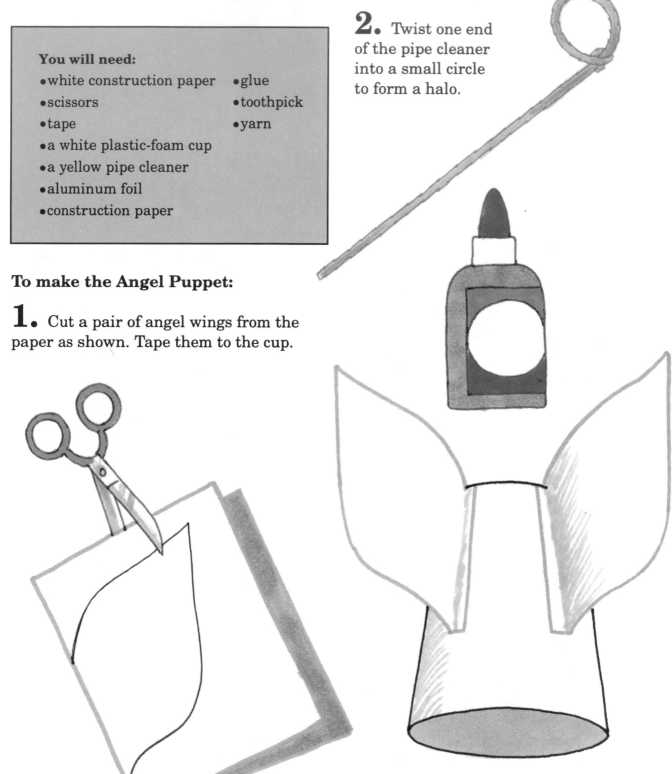

You will need:
- white construction paper
- scissors
- tape
- a white plastic-foam cup
- a yellow pipe cleaner
- aluminum foil
- construction paper
- glue
- toothpick
- yarn

To make the Angel Puppet:

1. Cut a pair of angel wings from the paper as shown. Tape them to the cup.

2. Twist one end of the pipe cleaner into a small circle to form a halo.

3. Cut off a 7-inch square of aluminum foil and squeeze it into a ball around the stem of the halo. Make the ball smooth by covering it with another small piece of foil. This is the angel's head.

4. Poke a hole with a toothpick in the bottom of the cup. Push the pipe cleaner through the hole. Use yarn and construction paper to make facial features and hair.

5. Put the cup over your hand and hold on to the pipe cleaner to use the puppet.

With these cookies, you'll love doing windows.

Stained-Glass Cookies

You will need:

- a 12-ounce package bittersweet chocolate chips
- 8 tablespoons (1 stick) butter or margarine
- a 12-ounce package colored mini-marshmallows
- ½ cup chopped nuts (optional)
- ½ cup shredded coconut
- a double boiler*
- a mixing spoon
- aluminum foil

* To make a double boiler, find two saucepans that fit inside one another. Add water to the bottom pan until it is filled ⅓ of the way.

To make Stained-Glass Cookies:

1. *Ask a grown-up to help you* melt the chocolate and margarine together in a double boiler over medium heat.

2. Cut four pieces of aluminum foil, each 12 inches by 4 inches. Sprinkle a layer of coconut on the foil.

3. Remove pan from heat and stir marshmallows, nuts, and remaining coconut into the chocolate.

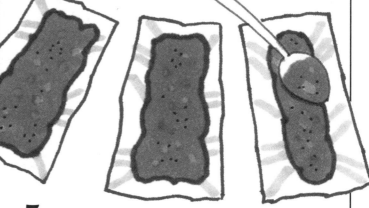

4. Spread the mixture evenly onto the four pieces of foil. Use a spoon to mold it into log shapes.

5. Carefully roll each piece of foil closed, secure the ends, and refrigerate for 45 minutes or until it has hardened. Slice as needed.

These cookies won't "hang" around too long!

Christmas Wreath Cookies

You will need:

- 1 teaspoon vanilla
- 3½ cups corn-flakes cereal
- green food coloring
- red cinnamon candies
- ½ cup butter
- thirty marshmallows
- a saucepan
- waxed paper
- a mixing spoon

2. Stir the cornflakes into the marshmallow mixture until all of the cereal is coated.

To make Christmas Wreath Cookies:

1. *Ask a grown-up to help you* melt the vanilla, butter, and marshmallows together in a pan on low heat. Once the mixture is creamy, stir in green food coloring until it is the shade you want. Remove the pan from the heat.

3. Once the mixture is cool enough to touch, rub a little butter on your fingers and use your hands to form the coated cereal into wreath shapes. Stick on red cinnamon candies as berries. Place the cookies on waxed paper to cool.

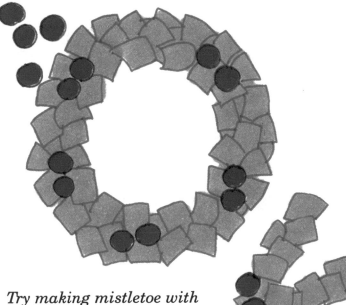

Try making mistletoe with the coated cereal mixture!

This just might be the reason Santa's so round.

Mrs. Claus's Favorite Fudge

You will need:
- an 8-ounce jar of marshmallow
- 1½ cups sugar
- ⅔ cup (a 5-ounce can) evaporated milk
- ¼ cup butter or margarine
- 2 cups (12 ounces) semisweet chocolate chips
- 1 teaspoon vanilla extract
- chopped nuts (optional)
- an 8-inch-square greased pan
- a large saucepan

2. *Ask a grown-up to help you* stir the mixture constantly over medium heat. Bring it to a boil. Let it boil five minutes while stirring constantly. Remove the pan from the heat and add in the chocolate chips. Stir until the chips are melted. Mix in the vanilla extract and nuts.

To make Mrs. Claus's Favorite Fudge:

1. Add the marshmallow, sugar, evaporated milk, and butter to the saucepan.

3. Pour the mixture into the greased pan. Chill until firm, then cut into bite-size pieces.

It'll look too good to eat, but take a bite.

Graham Cracker Holiday House

2. Using the sugar paste, glue four whole graham crackers to form a square for the base of the house. Glue a half of a cracker on top for the ceiling. Glue on two or more cracker halves for the roof and fill in the peak with candies.

You will need:
- water
- a bowl
- a spoon
- a plastic-foam meat tray
- graham crackers
- 1 cup confectioner's sugar
- assorted candy for decoration (gumdrops, chocolates, or licorice)

To make the Graham Cracker Holiday House:

1. In a bowl, mix the confectioner's sugar and a bit of water to form a smooth, thick paste. Spread a thin layer of the sugar paste on the bottom of the plastic-foam tray.

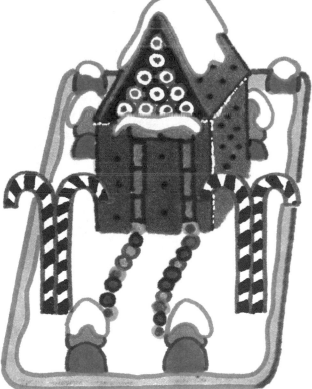

Other decorating ideas:

Candy canes make tasty trees; a gumdrop walk is colorful; the sugar paste can be dripped on the roof or windows to look like fallen snow.

Here's an "eye-popping" Christmas card for that special relative or friend!

Pop-Up Christmas Card

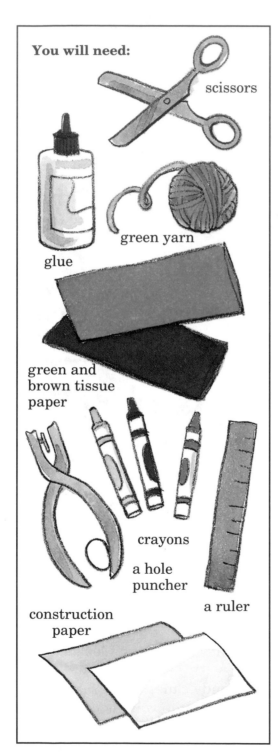

You will need:

scissors

green yarn

glue

green and brown tissue paper

crayons

a hole puncher

a ruler

construction paper

To make the Pop-Up Christmas Card:

1. Cut five pieces of the green tissue paper in the following sizes: 2 inches by 8 inches, 3 inches by 8 inches, 4 inches by 8 inches, 5 inches by 8 inches, and 6 inches by 8 inches. Fold each piece like a fan. The folds should be parallel to the short edges of the paper. Each pleat should be about a ½ inch wide.

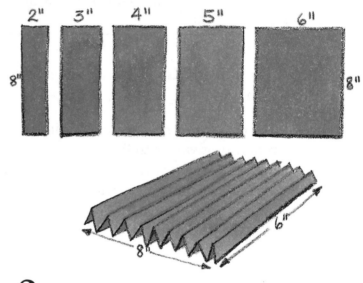

2. Fold all the fans in half. Lightly glue the center edges together to form semicircles.

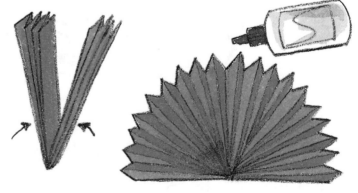

3. Fold a piece of construction paper in half; then open it up. Glue the semicircles to the fold in a tree shape. For the tree trunk, cut a piece of the brown tissue paper 2 inches by 8 inches. Follow the folding instructions in steps 1 and 2. Glue the brown semicircle beneath the tree.

4. Cut a star out of yellow paper, and glue it above the tree.

HOW LOVELY ARE YOUR BRANCHES!

MERRY CHRISTMAS !!!

LOVE, KYLE

OH CHRISTMAS TREE, OH CHRISTMAS TREE....

5. Using crayons, decorate the front and inside of the card with a Christmas message.

6. Close the card, and punch a hole in the side with the hole puncher. Tie a bow made of green yarn through the hole to hold the card shut.

Everyone loves a surprise in the mail.

Christmas Tree Card

4. Fold the paper in half so that one long side of the triangle is on the crease. Cut out the triangle, but do not cut on the crease. This is your card.

You will need:
- colored construction paper
- scissors
- glitter (if you have it)
- glue
- a ruler
- a pencil

To make the Christmas Tree Card:

1. Draw a 4½-inch horizontal line on a piece of construction paper. (Make the line light enough to erase.)

2. Make a mark in the center of the line (at 2¼ inches), and then from that point, draw a vertical line 5 inches long.

5. Erase the pencil marks and decorate the tree using cutout paper decorations, glue, and glitter.

6. Let it dry, then write a message to a friend inside.

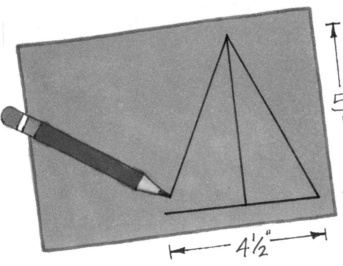

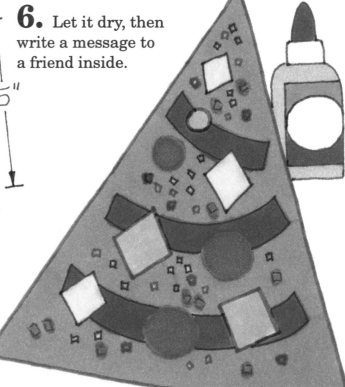

3. Connect the ends of the first line to the top of the 5-inch line. You will have a triangle.

and Envelope

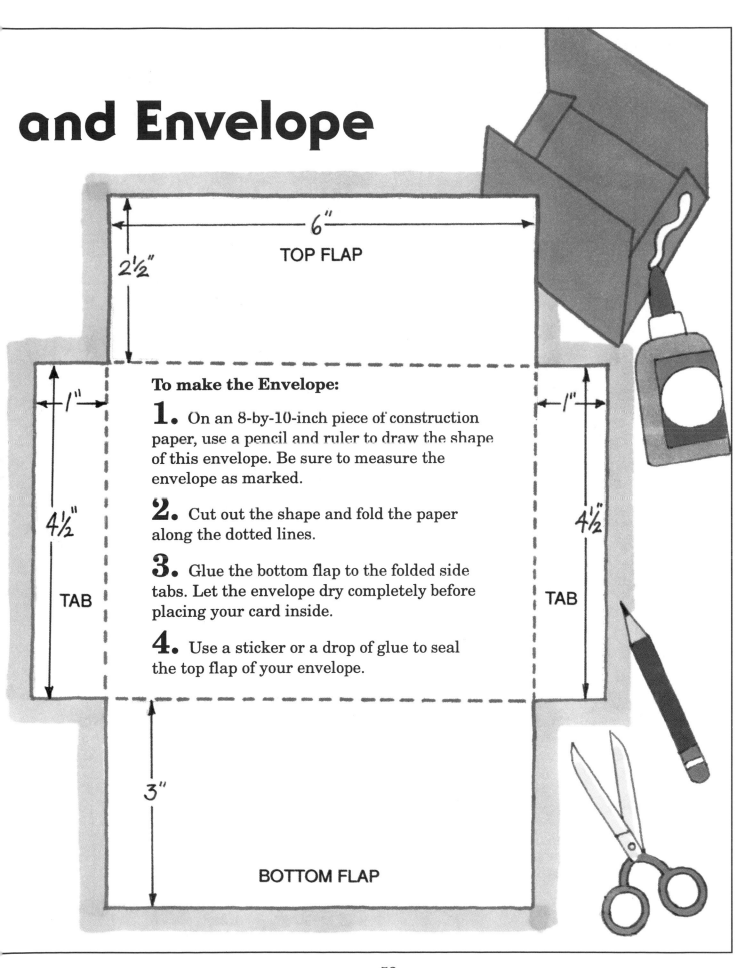

6"

TOP FLAP

2½"

1"

1"

4½"

4½"

TAB

TAB

To make the Envelope:

1. On an 8-by-10-inch piece of construction paper, use a pencil and ruler to draw the shape of this envelope. Be sure to measure the envelope as marked.

2. Cut out the shape and fold the paper along the dotted lines.

3. Glue the bottom flap to the folded side tabs. Let the envelope dry completely before placing your card inside.

4. Use a sticker or a drop of glue to seal the top flap of your envelope.

3"

BOTTOM FLAP

Mark off the days till Christmas with this easy-to-make advent calendar.

Countdown to

You will need:

a large sheet of poster board

markers

scissors

white paper

glue

a black marker

colored felt

To make the Advent Calendar:

1. Using the markers on the poster board, draw a fireplace with a fire burning in it.

2. Cut out twenty-five circles from the white paper. Label them 1 to 25 with the black marker. Glue them in order on the fireplace.

Christmas!

3. Cut out twenty-five stockings from different-colored felt.

4. On December 1, twenty-five days before Christmas, tape or glue a stocking over the circle labeled 25. On December 2, glue a stocking over the circle labeled 24, and so on.

Bird Feeder

You will need:
- an empty half-gallon cardboard milk carton
- scissors
- heavy string or twine
- a tree twig or stick about 1 foot long
- bird seed

To make the Bird Feeder:

1. Rinse out the milk carton and let it dry.

2. Cut out two squares, each about 4 inches, on opposite sides of the milk carton.

3. Use the scissors to poke a small hole about a ½ inch under each square. Slide the twig through the holes.

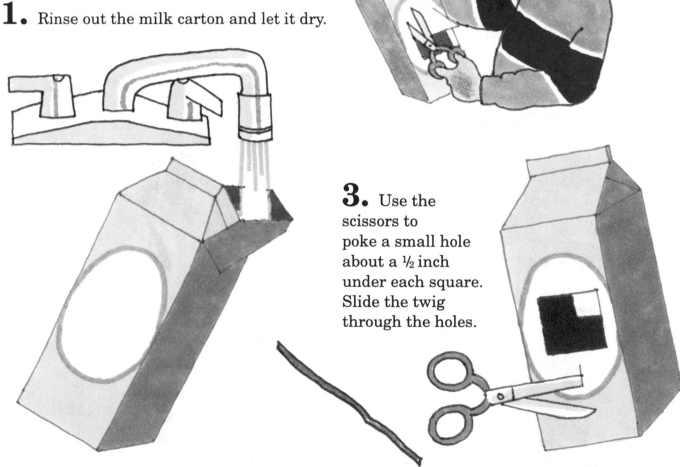

5. Hang the birdfeeder outside on a tree branch. Choose a branch that you can see from a window in your house, and watch the birds come by to eat!

4. For a hanger, make a hole through the top of the milk carton. String a 2-foot-long piece of twine through the hole, and tie the ends together securely. Pour about 3 inches of birdseed into the feeder.

Don't forget to refill the feeder when it's empty.

This sweet-smelling gift is easy to make, but it takes a long time to dry. So be sure to make it in advance.

A Pomander

You will need:
- a thin-skinned, unbruised, orange
- 1 ounce whole cloves
- 1 teaspoon cinnamon powder
- a 2-ounce packet of orrisroot powder* (optional)
- 1 yard of ribbon (not more than ¼ inch wide)
- two straight pins
- two 12-inch strips of paper (the same width as the ribbon)
- three pieces of 12-by-12-inch tissue paper
- a small paper bag
- a medium-size mixing bowl
- a small skewer
- a mixing spoon

*found in most health food stores

To make the Pomander:

1. Wrap the strips of paper and pin them to the top of the orange. Wrap the paper down the sides of the orange and secure them to the bottom with the other pin.

2. Poke a hole through the skin of the orange with the skewer. Push a clove into the hole up to its head. Continue piercing and filling each hole with a clove until all four sections are covered.

3. Mix the cinnamon and orrisroot in the bowl.

4. Remove the pins and paper strips, and roll the orange in the mixture on waxed paper until it is completely coated.

6. Place the orange in the paper bag and store it in a dry, dark place for a month. It is important to let the orange dry completely or it will rot.

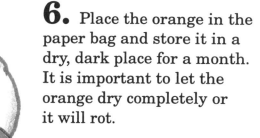

5. Place the orange on three layers of tissue paper and wrap up the orange by twisting the paper at each end.

7. Tie the ribbons to the pomander as shown to make a bow and a loop.

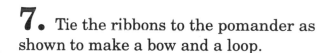

This box is so special it can be the gift!

Gift-Wrap Gift

You will need:
- poster board (14 by 14 inches)
- colored cellophane (found in hobby shops)
- glue
- a pencil
- a ruler
- scissors
- tape

To make the Gift-Wrap Gift:

1. Draw a horizontal line 12 inches long across the top, back side of the poster board. Make a mark in the middle of the line (at 6 inches). From that middle point, draw a 10¼-inch-long vertical line.

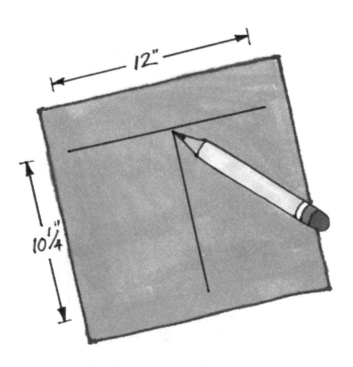

2. Connect the ends of the first line drawn to the bottom of the vertical line. You will have a triangle.

3. Make marks at middle points of the lines that make up the triangle. Connect the lines as shown to form four triangles within the large triangle.

4. Add ½-inch tabs as shown by the red lines.

5. Cut along the red lines and fold along the black lines. Cut out a triangle on the top flap, and tape a piece of cellophane to the inside of the poster board.

6. Glue the side flaps together. Tuck the top folds into the sides of the base.

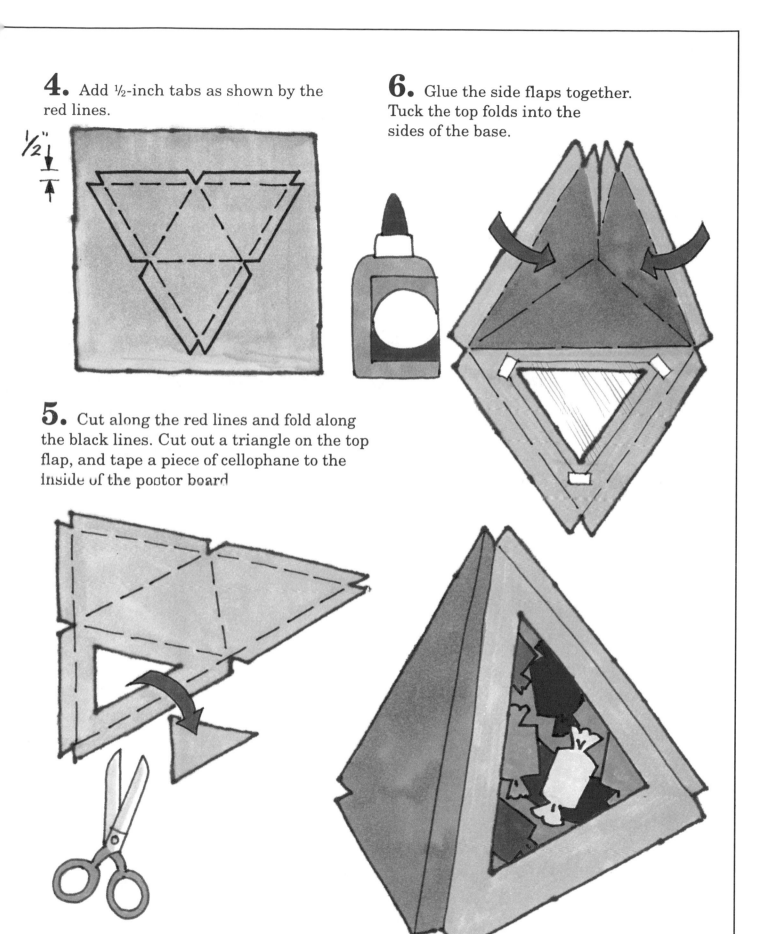

Coupon Book

3. Make a colorful cover for the coupon book, and staple the coupons together as shown.

You will need:
- construction paper
- markers or crayons
- a ruler
- scissors
- a stapler

To make the Coupon Book:

1. Cut out several 5-by-3-inch sheets of paper.

2. On each piece of paper, write a promise to do something especially nice for the person receiving this gift.

Title Index

Subject Index